SAVED BY A BUG

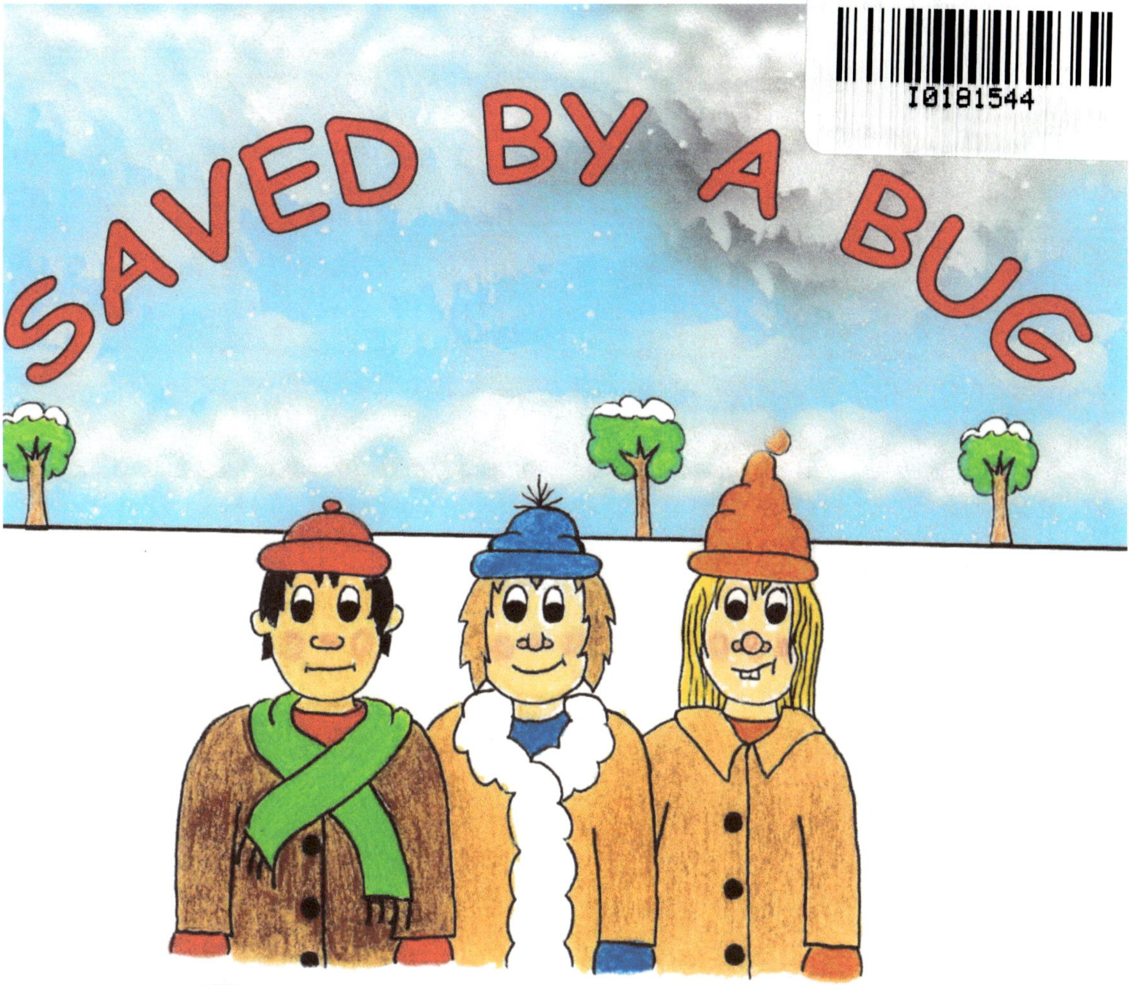

THE STORY BEHIND THE GAME "PUNCH BUGGY"

STORY AND ILLUSTRATIONS BY
RICK C. GARCIA

Wagoner Oklahoma

© 2025 Rick C. Garcia

All rights reserved. No part of this book may be reproduced, distributed, or transmitted in any form or by any means, including photocopying, recording, or other electronic or mechanical methods, without prior written permission from the publisher, except in the case of brief quotations for review purposes.
All characters, storylines, and artwork are the property of Rick C. Garcia.

Published by AZ Literary Press
An imprint of AZ Entertainment Group LLC

ISBN: 978-1-947035-65-2

For inquiries, including bulk orders of 100 or more, please contact:

AZ Entertainment Group LLC
PO BOX 854
Wagoner, OK 74477-0854

Email: info@az-entertainmentllc.com
Website: www.az-entertainmentllc.com

Printed in the United States of America

For my daughter, Rikki Lynn,
who can spot a bug from a quarter mile away.

As told to me by Matthew James Garcia.

In the town where I grew up, winters weren't very grim. It rarely ever snowed, power didn't go out, pipes didn't burst, and we never missed any school.

Then came a winter I'll never forget: the power was knocked out, pipes burst, and we were out of school for a whole week!

After several days of icy twenty-degree weather, my two best friends, John and Cyril, and I waded through the snow to the lake in the back of our neighborhood to see if it had frozen over. It had.

Because it rarely snows here, we didn't own sleds or ice skates or any of the fancy toys that kids up north have for winter.

Wanting to be able to take advantage of our lake being frozen over, we came up with the idea to walk onto the frozen lake and build ourselves a swimming deck for summer.

At the time, there were houses being built around the lake, so John, Cyril, and I took boards and nails from the job sites and used them to build our deck.

We walked across the ice to the only trees grouped close enough together for us to build our deck. We built the deck roughly five feet above the ice and then nailed four short boards down one side of a tree to use as a ladder.

Six months later, when summer finally came around, we rode our bicycles to the lake to try out the deck. Without hesitation, we dropped our bikes, ran for the water, dove in, and raced each other to the deck.

Our deck was roughly a hundred yards out. A pretty good swim for a bunch of eleven-year-olds.

When we made it to the deck, we saw a wasp-covered nest—WASPS!—on the second board of the ladder.

John was deathly allergic to bees.

When the wasps saw us, they came off the nest and started swarming around us.

We made a quick decision to swim back to shore.

That hundred-yard swim to the deck was now turning into a two-hundred-yard swim! Since we had raced each other, we were already pretty tired, so the swim back to the shore was going to be a real challenge.

Around halfway back to shore, I started feeling a burning ache in my arms and my shoulders began to throb. I was tired and becoming somewhat panicky thinking I might not be able to make it. I was terrified of drowning. We all were.

John, who was trailing behind Cyril and me, yelled out, "Hey you guys, wait up for me!"

This definitely wasn't a good time for hanging out, so I kept on swimming.

Then John yelled, "Help me you guys! I can't make it!"

John's plea for help sent shivers throughout my entire body, like I was suddenly swimming in ice-cold water. He began to scream out for us to please come back and help him. He was in full panic mode.

I didn't know what to do. I'm no lifeguard, I can't swim fifty yards with someone in tow, and besides that, I was struggling myself. So I did the only thing I could think of. I encouraged him.

"Come on, John, it's not that much further. You can make it."

"Please you guys, don't let me drown!" His plea echoed across the lake.

I kept swimming. John went silent.

John's pleas for help did not fall on deaf ears; I heard every word of it. It's a sound that still haunts me, but I was in no position to help him, because I was struggling too.

Then, as if from the grave, John screamed out again, "I can touch!"

I tried to touch, but there wasn't a bottom to touch, so I had to keep swimming.

Cyril and I were totally exhausted when we got to shore. We laid on the ground, huffing and puffing, trying to catch our breaths. When we got up and looked out over the lake, we could see John's face barely poking out above the surface of the water.

John rested, got his second wind and swam to shore.

We all made it!

There had been this rumor going around about some teenagers stealing a car that winter, and driving it out on the frozen lake, cracking the ice, and barely escaping with their lives.

Later on that same summer, our lake was drained so the county could repair the dam, and sure enough, sitting in the mud, in the exact spot where John was able to touch, was a Volkswagen Beetle, a car people referred to as a "Bug."

John was always jokingly saying, "I was fleeing a bee, and was saved by a Bug!"

    After that day at the lake, every time John would see a Volkswagen Beetle, he would punch me and Cyril in the arm to remind us that we had abandoned him that day, and it was the Volkswagen Beetle, not us, that had saved his life. And of course, we couldn't punch him back.

    Soon, John's reminder to us became something all the kids in the neighborhood started doing whenever they spotted a Volkswagen Beetle. The first to spot one could punch a friend in the arm and say, "Saved by a Bug, can't hit back," and the friend couldn't punch them back.

    It wasn't very long before we started calling the Volkswagen Beetle a "Slug Bug," or "Punch Buggy." It depended on which side of the neighborhood you lived on.

As the years rolled by, the kids from our neighborhood started moving away to other towns, cities, and states. No doubt they taught their new friends our "Saved by a Bug" game, because now, EVERYONE has played it: You've played it, your kids have played it, and it's something fun to do when you're bored in the car.

The thing is, nobody seems to know how this game originated, or the story behind it.

Now, you know!

Acknowledgments

    Thank you to: Christine, Lillyana, and Ariana for your support.

    Special thanks to: Rene, Riva, and Rona for putting up with me.

About the Author

Rick C. Garcia lives in Fayetteville, North Carolina. You can write him at:

7514 Paxton Drive
Fayetteville, NC 28303

www.ingramcontent.com/pod-product-compliance
Lightning Source LLC
LaVergne TN
LVHW072102070426
835508LV00002B/238